A COLLECTION OF COMIC SATIRICAL POETRY

By Jim Hubler
Author ~ Songwriter ~ Guitar Owner ~
Part-time Poet

A Description Of My Poetry

First of all, let me say, some of my critics say my work is not really poetry at all. Some say it is merely 'Tripe', others say it's 'Over-ripe Tripe', while still others have even gone so far as to call my works a criminal misuse of pen and paper, a word processor and the English language. Some have threatened to start proceedings to cancel my 'poetic license'. Well, so much for critics.

I rely heavily on the most authoritative reference book on poetry that I have ever owned – "Poetry For Dummies", and I feel it was written for someone just like me. According to this wonderful book of poetry reference, my poetry would be best described as follows:

Genre: It is a blend of comedy, lyric poetry, satire, sarcasm, light verse, and just plain nonsense. As for the lyric part of this genre description, I should explain. At times I blend Country Song lyrics with Rap, and there are those that call this 'Crap'.
Its purpose: To make people laugh a little, the world needs to lighten up. Though I realize it will probably accomplish little, I do make some critical social commentary from time to time.

My reasoning is this, why should the joke always be on us? Some of the biggies need to learn to take a joke once in awhile. Most of them tend to take themselves much too seriously; they can be replaced. Also, in most cases, we, the general public, are paying their wages plus much more, very often, too much more.

Dedication

This Poetry Collection is respectfully dedicated to Professional Politicians and those aspiring to be Professional Politicians. Their performances are usually quite entertaining, and the long-lasting effects of their performances are often felt long after they have left the stage of public office.

It cannot be denied that acting and politics share many similarities. The politicians must endeavor to act out the role to which they have been cast to play. Most play it to the limits of their expertise.

While motion pictures, TV, etc. all have their grand achievement awards for best performances etc., sadly it seems there are no such awards for Politicians. In view of this, I would respectfully suggest forming some sort of achievement awards program for Politicians. Perhaps there could be awards for Best Stage Performance, Best Acting, Best Stage Presence, Best Hair and even Best Dressed. As well there might be another category for 'Best Stand-up Comedy' - many could qualify for this one! In any case, I feel that the opportunity to present awards and recognition for our dedicated public servants should not be overlooked. America, let's give them what they deserve!

Contents

Poetic License Revocation 1
What If? 2
Everything Is On The Table 4
Default Of Whom? 6
Kicking The Can On Down The Road 8
Cutting Government Spending 10
I Had A Dream 12
They Have A Funny Way At The TSA 14
Down South On The Border 16
Governmental Spending Habits 18
Required Reading 20
Dysfunction Junction 22
Verbal Dueling 24
Long Time Public Servant 26
More Political Debate 28
Inexperienced Politicians 29
A Governmental Quick Fix 31
Mud-Slinging USA ~ Politics Today 33
Our Broken Government 35
Newscasters And Analysts 37
Election Coverage USA 39
I Thought We Had Learned Our Lesson 41
Lack Of Experience Can Sometimes Be A Plus 43
It's A Crude Awakening 44
The Gusher In The Gulf 46
Mishap In The Gulf 48
A Really Crude Awakening 49
Wasted Water, A Wasted Way Of Life 51

The Great Debate.. 53
Understanding Politics 55
The Political Game... 57
Coming Close 58
Voting Absentee... 59
The Good Side Of Deep Snow............................ 61
Too Many Snouts In The Trough........................ 63
Campaign Promises.. 65
The Obscene High Of Campaign Costs 66
Fiscal Restraint.. 68
Front Cover Of The CAGW's* "Congressional Pig
Book".. 70
The Bucket And The Hog ~ Part 1...................... 72
The Bucket And The Hog ~ Part 2...................... 75
The Bucket And The Hog ~ Part 3...................... 78
Who Is Gonna Bail US Out?............................... 81
We Are All In This Mess Together ~ Part 1 82
We Are All In This Mess Together ~ Part 2 85
I'm Afraid The Good Old Days Are Coming Back 87
Full-time Part-time 89
I Have Outlived All My Savings........................... 91
The Litter Box Of Life 93
I Still Have The Biggest Part............................... 94
The Ballad Of Bad Bernie Madoff ~ Part 1 95
The Ballad Of Bad Bernie Madoff ~ Part 2 97
The Ballad Of Bad Bernie Madoff ~ Part 3 99
The Ballad Of Bad Bernie Madoff ~ Part 4 101
The High Cost Of Executive Expertise................. 103
Alibis And Lies 105
A Tribute To Two Wranglers.............................. 107

Extracurricular Activities..109
A DVD Dilemma 111
Saturday Night SOB (Sunday Morning Saint).......113
The Way It Seems To Be At The SEC....................115
Web Surfing At The SEC...116
Attorneys With Ambition ~ Part 1 118
Attorneys With Ambition ~ Part 2.........................120
Thanks To Our Attorneys..122
Success At Last 124

Poetic License Revocation

Some say that there's a movement on
to revoke my poetic license.

To those I say, "Please don't act in haste.
With some deliberation, you may well find
that a weirdly warped poetic mind
is indeed a terrible thing to waste."

What If?

We are plagued by politicians, each with their own agenda,
each trying to outdo his predecessor by being a bigger spender.
Many analysts agree, and say they most surely do suspect
that bunglers ruined a great system, and nearly have it wrecked.

What if our Country had more Statesmen, and far fewer Politicians?
Then, perhaps they could work together, and accomplish their missions.
They would worry less of party loyalties, and of party affiliations
and conduct business more civilly, with fewer verbal altercations.

Then they could concentrate more, on doing the job they're elected for.
Just do the job, obey the rules, and in the world's eyes not appear as fools.
Maybe then they could knuckle down and start working full years.
Start working for the good of the country, not their campaign financiers.

What If? (cont.)

Politicians are preoccupied with re-election and affiliations,
while Statesmen are concerned with the good of future generations.
What if we had fewer Politicians, and more Statesmen to take their place?
And Statesmen cared more for our Country, than winning a political race?

A true Statesman is a rarity, a type of person you seldom see.
What if we had more Statesmen, in our great land of the free?
If this were to happen, I really think there would be no doubt.
We would gain the respect of the world, and regain our former clout.

Everything Is On The Table

Congress was working frantically,
trying to cure our Nation's ills,
hunting ways to cut back on spending,
so we can pay our Country's bills.

They said, "Everything is on the table.
We will make cuts anywhere we're able.
It's going to make some folks queasy.
It's serious business and won't be easy."

Congress had been working night and day.
Some members acted uptight and spooky.
Then there came an unusual proposal,
that sounded strange and somewhat kooky.

A young Freshman Congressman,
who only recently had been elected
made an obscene suggestion,
and almost got ejected.

The Speaker said, "What's that you say?
You're suggesting cutting Congressional pay?
Young man, surely you can't be serious.
Son, these long hours have made you delirious!"

The proceedings got unruly,
and soon started to unravel.

Everything Is On The Table (cont.)

When the Speaker called for order,
and banged his official gavel.

What happened next, you might well guess,
he called for an extremely long recess.
That obscene proposal, we understand,
went in a file called, 'Fantasy Land'.

The Speaker said, "What's that you say?
You're suggesting cutting Congressional pay?
Young man, surely you can't be serious.
Son, these long hours have made you delirious!"

When things settled down a little more,
the Speaker once more took the floor.
He said, "Everything's on the table
and we'll cut spending where we're able."

But that Freshman's obscene proposal
 was just a little bit too much.
For we all know in Washington,
there are some things you just don't touch.

Default Of Whom?

They like to blame the possibility
of our Nation's Debt Default
for the lack of US dollar
in our country's Treasury Vault.

They can't agree on cut cap and spend.
Some just want to borrow more
from anyone who would lend;
even those from far off-shore.

They stomp out of meetings,
which then abruptly end.
Never giving any thought
to the type of message this might send.

They all feel they are qualified
to run our great land.
But many think them not capable
of running a peanut stand.

Legislators want to spend more.
That's what they're elected for.
The Government could easily pay
if debt limits raise right away.

I predict we'll never see the day
Congress would ever mention a word

Default Of Whom? (cont.)

that they might not receive their pay.
Now that would be quite absurd.

While they're quarreling and debating,
We are in danger of a lower credit rating.
I wish they'd learn to play well together
and get over their jealousy and hating.

They talk about cutting Government spending.
We hear this talked about each day.
But we have not heard one single word,
about cutting Congressional pay.

My heart goes out to Congress.
They've been working nights and some weekends.
They can't agree on our country's debt limit,
on the money our Government spends.

But I do think in fairness
to a Legislator and his staff,
For those nights and weekend work,
they should be paid time and a half.

In lots of other places,
they would be paid double time.
But we should avoid reckless spending
of the American taxpayer's dime.

Kicking The Can On Down The Road

Our National Debt is quite obese.
We must find a way to 'slim it'.
There's no other workable way.
We should pass a debt ceiling limit.

They engage in long debates
about reducing our National Debt.
But talking about it seems to be
about as far as they ever get.

The talk the talk, but do not do it.
They're only giving it 'lip service'
which makes credit rating agencies
real uptight and quite nervous.

They want to sidestep the problem,
kick the can on down the road.
Saddle future generations
with an obscene big debt load.

Some of the bills they want to pass
have no real meaning, we are finding.
For, to those elected in the future
they would not be valid or binding.

It's mostly smoke and mirrors,
some mathematical sleight of hand,

Kicking The Can On Down The Road (cont.)

written in complicated language,
most folks just would not understand.

When they talk of debt reduction,
and this taking a total of ten years,
they are being somewhat less than candid,
and this confirms my biggest fears.

They want to sidestep the problem,
kick the can on down the road.
Saddle future generations
with an obscene big debt load.

Cutting Government Spending

They talk of cutting Government spending.
We hear this every day.
But we haven't heard one single word,
about cutting Congressional pay.

Congress is in a constant squabble,
not taking care of business there at hand.
They'll keep on bitching and hating
'til they ruin the credit rating of our land.

If they're not capable of running things any more,
perhaps their jobs should be outsourced offshore.
I don't intend to sound harsh or mean,
Let's replace 'em with some high tech machine.

We don't care who is King of the Clubhouse.
Just get together and work as one!
We don't give a damn about political parties
Just get to work and get 'er done.

If I don't get my Social Security check,
I'm gonna feel like wringing someone's neck.
Our Legislators had better get a grip
before they let our credit rating slip.

Yes, we get the strangest feeling.
These folks don't want a debt ceiling.

Cutting Government Spending (cont.)

They want to use that credit card until it's maxed.
Then people will learn the meaning of being taxed.

When this happens, times could get real hard,
 unless someone sends 'em another credit card.
But if our spenders got too loose and relaxed,
It wouldn't be long 'til that credit card was maxed.

There was a time when we were 'on top of the
heap',
But sometimes good credit rating is hard to keep.
It seems those who regulate our country's spending
keep piling up debt with no thought of ending.

I Had A Dream

I drifted off to sleep last night, in my chair with the
TV playing.
The late night news was showing what the
Politicians were saying.
The debates were getting heated, how our Nation's
in debt so deep.
But in spite of all this bad news, I drifted off in
peaceful sleep.

I had a peaceful dream, a dream that seemed so real,
that our Legislators got together and worked out a
budget deal.
And they all seemed to like each other, working
together oh so well.
And they all smiled and talked in civil tones,
without one single yell.

They'd put aside party loyalties, and worked for the
good of the nation.
And what's more, they said they'd stay and work,
forgetting that vacation.
They all really acted in word and deed as if they
were true Statesmen
not worried about re-election, more concerned with
the next generation.

In my peaceful dream, ongoing, there was comfort
in just knowing.

I Had A Dream (cont.)

That both parties worked together, not acting like
DC ideologues.
When the political news came on TV, it brought me
back to reality.
With manners like hungry hogs, they were fighting
like cats and dogs.

When I awoke, things weren't at all like they had
seemed.
Politicians co-operating, was only something I had
dreamed.
But with our National Debt, nearly bursting at the
seams,
the thought of level-headed thinking was in my
wildest dreams.

I was jolted back to reality, when the morning news
came on the air.
And I found that I had been only dreaming in my
favorite chair.
The reality of things in DC ain't one damn bit like
my dream.
They don't play well with others; that's just how
they make it seem.

They Have A Funny Way At The TSA

My girlfriend claims I am a groper.
In my own defense, I would like to say
you really haven't been thoroughly groped
'til you've been groped by the TSA.

Now the word is out, 'round Frisco Bay.
The boys go to the airport every day.
They have no intention of leaving town.
They just show up to get 'patted down'.

At that perhaps I really should explain
All being screened do not complain
One said, "Sir, I think your screening is fine!"
"How many times may I go through the line?"

These days we are hearing numerous reports.
Agents seem preoccupied with shorts.
But, these little things should be overlooked.
It makes things safer for the flight you booked.

Yes, the TSA is diligently doing its part,
and has the flying public's welfare at heart.
So let's be forgiving if Agents act in error,
for it's a vital part of 'The War On Terror'.

Yes, my girlfriend claims I am a groper.
Again in my defense, I would like to say

They Have A Funny Way At The TSA (cont.)

you really haven't been thoroughly groped
'til you've been groped by the TSA.

Down South On The Border

To better secure our country,
and better maintain law and order,
We were building a high-tech border fence
down on our southern border.

In management, there was indecision.
Some said the system lacked precision.
It was claimed by some with political clout
the fences couldn't keep illegals out.

When government leaders disagree,
a bad decision often follows.
Now, they've pulled the plug on the project
after spending ten billion dollars.

We've shut down the high-tech border fence
'cause some crossed and the monitors missed 'em.
Now, we are saving a bunch of money,
border crossings are on the 'honor system'.

Now, we could patrol our borders
using Reserves and National Guard.
But we don't want to seem severe,
or do anything harsh or hard.

And if a member of our border patrol
stops bad guys with well- aimed lead,

Down South On The Border (cont.)

the Border Agents go to prison
when the outlaws should go instead.

When jailed Border Agents' freedoms are gone,
for maintaining law and order,
we wonder whose side the law is on,
down on our Southern Border.

But if we were to secure the border,
there's one thing clearly understood.
We'd have some severe shortages
which, for sure, would not be good.

We'd need 'Mexican laughing tobacco'
and pharmaceuticals for our 'high'.
For the reason it all keeps coming North,
it's what modern Americans like to buy.

We want no international incidents.
We don't want border fights.
Will the last one leaving Mexico
make sure you turned out the lights?

Governmental Spending Habits

Some say the government is
spending money like drunk sailors.
That's an insult to drunk sailors I have known.
For the government is spending,
other people's money,
while drunk sailors only spend their own.

The government spends like there's no tomorrow.
When they overdo, they go offshore and borrow.
Their spending habits are kinda scary.
It's like they've found the 'money fairy'.
Or, like they have a 'money dog' they squeeze.
They're spending billions anytime they please.

Some say the government is
spending money like drunk sailors.
That's an insult to drunk sailors I have known.
For the government is spending,
other people's money,
while drunk sailors only spend their own.

 Now, here's a thought, if it ain't too late.
Here's a group the government could emulate.
They could spend money like drunken sailors,
Whose spending habits are quite well known.
Yes, if our leaders spent money like drunk sailors,
They'd not borrow, but would only spend their own.

Governmental Spending Habits (cont.)

Some say the government is
spending money like drunk sailors.
That's an insult to drunk sailors I have known.
For the government is spending,
other people's money,
while drunk sailors only spend their own.

We're on a fiscal roller coaster ride.
The actual deficit numbers they'd like to hide.
I guess the solution to this fiscal mess
is to fire up the Treasury printing press.
Print another batch of promissory notes,
and claim things are better just to get the votes.

Required Reading

A new Congressional bill is needed
and should be drafted this very day.
It should be passed overwhelmingly
and put in practice without delay.
Make the Constitution required reading,
a thing our country is really needing,
for all those elected in our land,
and pass a test to prove they understand.

They should be told in such a way,
that it's in their mind and there to stay.
that if they disagree with any part,
don't take office, don't even start.
Our Constitution is not complicated
nor even hard to understand.
It's protections don't apply to a chosen few,
but to all those in our great land.

It's not meant for selective interpretation.
It applies the same throughout our Nation.
It's not an outdated document from back when..
It's a brilliant composition by fair-minded men..
Anyone that disregards this master set of rules
and thinks it outdated and composed by fools,
shouldn't be entrusted with authority,
or be elected in this land of the free!

Required Reading (cont.)

At the reading, all members must attend
and listen intently from start to end.
This patriotic procedure, required twice a year,
allowing no disturbance, so all could easily hear,
they all solemnly swear they will uphold
the Constitution of our great land.
But if they do not know its contents,
how could they possibly understand?

Dysfunction Junction

The wheels of our Government now move so slow
it seems at times that they barely function.
Perhaps we should re-name the place,
and just call it 'Dysfunction Junction'.

If I done my work that slowly,
and could not point to progress made,
I'd be expecting a pink slip
and I'd very likely not be paid.

But so many of these folks feel no shame
and point to others that are to blame.
These people need to 'get in the groove'
You'd need to set stakes to see 'em move.

They think they're doing great work
and see no possible reason for their rejection.
They are all campaigning in their spare time
anticipating their coming re-election.

If the wheels of Government move much slower,
credit rating agencies will move us a notch lower.
If our Government wheels are not functioning,
Perhaps our system needs restructuring.

In the past, the wheel that squeaked the loudest
was the wheel that always got more grease.

Dysfunction Junction (cont.)

But news of that wheel being taken off
should be in the next big press release.

Now our people have a problem understanding
all this juvenile squabbling and grandstanding.
It seems they put more value on party loyalty
than the common good of the Land of the Free.

Verbal Dueling

What with all the verbal dueling,
the debate was getting kind of grueling.
The younger politician hoped for an end to it
But the old pro politician wasn't about to quit.

No, the old pro wasn't thinking end
and he finally got his second wind.
He remembered some old political dirt
and brought up some things he knew could hurt.

By his silver tongue and well chosen words,
he had been re-elected many times before.
But now his constituents have noticed,
The Senator has lobbyist friends galore.

Now the voters just are not so sure
that the old pro's intentions are so pure.
He claims he wants to crusade on,
but things might be better with him gone.

Nowadays most every voter knows
it's because of those political pros
that our country is in the shape it's in.
Things might improve with an upstart win.

The upstart amateur office seeker
lacks experience and that is good.

Verbal Dueling (cont.)

For he is still honest and unconnected
and may just do what he says he would.

Yes, the longwinded career politician
will talk loud, debate and shout.
But a new breed of upstart office seekers
could just put the incumbents out!

Long Time Public Servant

He's not tall dark and handsome.
He's kind of short and dorky.
He has a nickname in the Senate
His colleagues call him 'Porky'.

When he's legislating on a bill,
there is one thing he will insist.
There must be 'pork' for his home district
included somewhere on that list.

He just likes to think of himself
as a modern day 'Robin Hood'
representing his constituents.
He's always up there doing good.

He's been in office for so long
some folks say he can't be beat.
For a long time it's been rumored,
he was born in that Senate seat.

But age just must make 'em better,
I think that's what they must suppose.
Some stay in office for so long
they can't see the end of their nose.

Yes, those long time Legislators
think that their time will never end.

Long Time Public Servant (cont.)

They stay in office 'til they must rely
so very much on their Depend®!

I'm too old to be an airline pilot
a trucker, soldier or a cop.
You know there are age restrictions.
Rules say the age when you must stop.

Some career politicians stay
'til they can barely breathe a breath.
Still making command decisions
on matters concerning life and death.

They are 'gentlemen of integrity'
On that fact they will insist.
And they won't accept a favor
from just 'any' old lobbyist.

Their campaigns for re-election,
never end, they are ongoing.
They intend to stay in office;
 a fact that's well worth knowing.

More Political Debate

It was once the game of gentlemen.
But now it's nothing of the sort.
Politicians fight like junk yard dogs.
Now, politics is a contact sport.

Take an old incumbent Senator,
who has been living like a Prince.
When some upstart says he'll win his seat,
he ain't so easy to convince.

Many years he's been his district's darling.
When challenged,
he comes out snarling.
His silver-tongued orations in the past,
have helped his career to last and last.

Now his constituents are short on basic needs.
Instead of words, they want actual deeds.
They recognize his rhetoric as more campaign crap,
And elect the upstart amateur in this flap.

This trend is on the upswing, all through the land.
Old incumbent politicians need to understand.
Voters suspect those with too many connections.
This may result in upsets in these elections.

Inexperienced Politicians

Once inexperienced politicians
were the butt of jokes and ridicule.
But nowadays they are in demand
and are popular as a rule.

Now there's a new phenomenon
that makes old politicians cuss.
Political inexperience, once a minus,
Nowadays is seen as a plus.

These newcomers to the political scene
don't owe their souls to lobbyists.
Nor a bunch of political IOUs,
to groups and people on a list.

So there's the chance it could be true
they will do the things they say they'll do.
This could happen, you can't tell.
This makes incumbents nervous as hell.

The people are tired of the same old song,
with very few different words.
Voters are thinking for themselves,
instead of running with the herds.

So, as they say 'bout a Broadway play,
"All new cast in a new production."

Inexperienced Politicians (cont.)

And if the play runs long enough,
we might see some debt reduction.

If the production has the right characters,
and if it does run long enough,
our land could see much improvement
with times not near as tough.

A Governmental Quick Fix

We can fix our broken government.
Here's what we need to do:
let Congress recess for fifty weeks.
they could do their work in two.

This would give them ample time
to plan their re-election,
and bond with their constituents,
and send pork in their direction.

They have been signing spending bills
most say they have not read.
Let's try something different.
Let's try something else instead.

I think what they're all needing
is a good course in speed-reading.
When they sign a bill they haven't read,
it gives us cause for fiscal dread.

It's like handing out a blank check;
one that has been signed.
So the recipients can just write in
the amounts they have in mind.

And if we want to save social security
so it will survive for you and me,

A Governmental Quick Fix (cont.)

put Congressional pensions in it
then it's bound to last, you'll see.

Then put these politician's health plan
in with ours in Medicare.
Why should their plan be different?
Everyone agrees it would be fair.

And then, of course, their pension plan
it ain't just good, it is the best.
Do they deserve a four year pension?
Why not twenty years like all the rest?

Well, we couldn't fix everything.
It would make politics too ordinary.
There'd be no incentive for personal gain
and the thought of that is scary!

Mud-Slinging USA ~ Politics Today

In the American game called politics,
if you're gonna play a major part,
there are some skills one must learn.
And then, perfect the art.

Some say that it's ill-mannered.
Some say it's vicious crud.
The skill that I am speaking of
is the art of slinging mud.

It's America's grand event,
with the excitement that it brings.
It happens every four years,
known as the 'Master Mud Slings'.

It's the All-American game
that's widely known as politics.
And there ain't no use in slinging mud,
unless at least a little sticks.

It's mud-slinging, yes, mud-slinging
think of all the votes it's bringing.
Casting innuendos, implying this and that,
candidates making charges tit for tat.

Always smile at your opponent
when you verbally attack.

Mud-Slinging USA ~ Politics Today (cont.)

Goad them in to saying things
that you know they can't take back.

Make allegations against the opponent
really close to election day.
Knowing there is no time,
to repudiate what you say.

The 'Mid-term Mud Slings' are exciting,
but not as much as the main event.
And sometimes, it's hard explaining
where all the campaign money went.

Yes, every four years in America,
they have to have a great big flap,
and spend lots of time and money,
out there throwing verbal crap.

Mud-slinging, yes, mud-slinging
done right here in the USA,
it is the national pastime,
that politicians love to play.

Our Broken Government

Some say our government is broken,
I think truer words were never spoken.
I'm sure it needs some fixing and repairs,
maybe even help from the man upstairs.

As soon as they take elected office,
they want to pay themselves some more.
It doesn't take long 'til they forget,
just who it is they're working for.

They all have some special interests,
that goes for each and every one.
They are listening to the lobbyists,
and nothing much is getting done.

Entice home folks with a little pork.
Bet your boots they're gonna take it.
If our country ain't quite broke just yet,
give 'em time, they will soon break it.

They won't listen to their constituents,
the very ones who sent 'em there.
For now that they've been elected,
they now no longer need to care.

We need to start a new production.
We need to start this very day,

Our Broken Government (cont.)

with an all new cast of characters,
as they say about a Broadway play.

We need some brand new talent.
Let's hold auditions for all parts.
We need to get our act together.
Yes, we all know it in our hearts.

For if our government isn't broken,
we know it's been badly bent.
Just wake up and smell the roses.
Oh, where has all the money went?

Newscasters And Analysts

It's newscasters and commentators,
and other like-minded souls,
who like to sway the elections,
before the voters reach the polls.

They claim they are 'unbiased'
when they're reporting on the facts.
But it's wise to watch 'em close,
during those public service acts.

We are all in this mess together.
We'll all have to suffer just the same.
We are all in this mess together,
and we'll all have to share in the blame.

They all do have their favorites,
and without a stutter or a stammer,
it's obvious who they're rooting for.
They're subtle as a big sledge hammer.

If you wonder who runs the country,
and who deciphers all those polls.
It's newscasters and commentators
and many more like-minded souls.

We are all in this mess together.
We'll all have to suffer just the same.

Newscasters And Analysts (cont.)

We are all in this mess together,
and we'll all have to share in the blame.

It's like we had all known down deep.
It's just like we had all supposed.
They try to sway the election,
before the polls are even closed.

So there's no need for big elections,
or huge campaigns that cost so much.
Let those nightly News Anchors do it;
it seems they have that special touch.

We are all in this mess together.
We'll all have to suffer just the same.
We are all in this mess together,
and we'll all have to share in the blame.

Election Coverage USA

Newscasters and some analysts,
all like to play a silly game.
They all project the likely winners,
each election it's the same.

They like to try to call the winners,
when just a few results are in.
They think they can see into the future,
that's the way it's always been.

If they'd just wait until it's over,
'til the votes are all computed,
they could report the wins with accuracy,
with fewer races being disputed.

They try to sway results their way,
with the facts they are 'distorting',
when just a very small percent,
of the precincts are reporting.

If I ever knew or heard of anyone,
that had been questioned in a poll,
it would then tend to reassure me,
and even serve to soothe my soul.

But no pollster has ever quizzed me,
nor anyone that I ever knew.

Election Coverage USA (cont.)

I have a sneaky feeling poll results,
are the work of that 'special few'.

So when you wonder who runs the country,
well, I think that really by and large,
it's the networks and newscasters.
They seem to be the ones in charge.

I Thought We Had Learned Our Lesson

A Japanese car maker had some safety problems,
and they tried to claim that this was something new.
But then it came to light, something was not right.
They had been hiding safety problems from public
view.

The more the buried records were found and
brought out,
the evidence was obvious, there could be no doubt.
It confirmed our worst suspicions, and our greatest
fears.
They'd had many problems and hid the facts for
years.

They were not the least forthcoming and evasive as
well.
But finally the truth came out, and someone had to
tell.
Congress said they were sneaky, and became
discerned.
But we should've known from a lesson previously
learned.

That they would do a thing so sneaky, really is no
revelation.
This is something we should remember together as a
nation.

I Thought We Had Learned Our Lesson (cont.)

We should have learned our lesson, from that
sneaky thing they done,
on December the seventh, back in nineteen forty-
one.

Lack Of Experience Can Sometimes Be A Plus

Now there's a new phenomenon
that here of late's been catching on.
It's enough to make old politicians cuss.

If new politicians lacked experience
it once was thought to be a minus.
But nowadays it seems to be a plus.

The inexperienced politician
just might well be a safer bet.
He's not an insider, well at least not yet.

He may still have some principles
and maybe not yet on the take
and happily married and not on the make.

So it might just be, that possibly
if elected, he or she might do right
not befriending lobbyists left and right.

Yes, the best politicians lack experience
and have principles oh so strong
but that changes when in office for too long.

It's A Crude Awakening

The markets all respond, to the daily price of crude
There is no doubt, the oil cartel, surely has us
screwed.
It's a crude awakening when you pull up to the
pumps.
Up thirty cents from yesterday, oh, how that price
jumps.

Yes, it's a crude awakening seeing prices on the
pumps.
When the wind blows in the desert, the price of
crude oil jumps.
They love our Yankee Dollars, they want all they
can grab
They've found the way to raise the price is through
the gift of gab.

Most of us still drive around, one person to a car.
While the bus goes by half-empty, it's common near
and far.
The oil cartel is thriving, as we all continue driving.
Buying gas at any cost, could our common sense be
lost?

Yes, it's a crude awakening seeing prices on the
pumps.
When the wind blows in the desert, the price of
crude oil jumps.

It's A Crude Awakening (cont.)

They love our Yankee Dollars, they want all they
can grab
They've found the way to raise the price is through
the gift of gab.

It's time to turn the tables, let's show 'em we ain't
fooling.
Ride the bus, even take the train, do some serious
car pooling
Let's slow the flow of Yankee Money, that they
have been taking in
Then it's gonna be their turn for a good old crude
awakening.

Yes, it's a crude awakening seeing prices on the
pumps.
When the wind blows in the desert, the price of
crude oil jumps.
They love our Yankee Dollars, they want all they
can grab
They've found the way to raise the price is through
the gift of gab.

The Gusher In The Gulf

Down deep in the Gulf of Mexico
a wrecked oil well is gushing crude.
It's ruining wildlife and ecology,
and making fish unfit for food.

It's killing off the wetlands
for as far as the eye can see.
It's causing massive problems,
in the Gulf Coast economy.

What produced one third of our seafood
now destroyed by fools spilling crude.
Those Louisiana fishermen
have now lost their livelihood.

They've been promised compensation
if this comes true it would be good.
The polluters promise full clean-up
and we feel they damn sure should.

The petrol folks will make things right
as the government does insist.
But the biggest fine they'll ever get
is like a light slap on the wrist.

We keep talking alternative energy
but it's just something on a list.
DC office doors are always open
to a petroleum lobbyist.

The Gusher In The Gulf (cont.)

They seem to have something special
that politicians all seem to need
And our legislators find the time
for doing them a real good deed.

If we'd regulate the regulators
we might stop this silly stuff.
We need to make them understand
the people have had quite enough.

But it's just noise, to the big oil boys
when our people complain and bitch.
For they all know, their pay will grow
and they'll keep getting super rich.

Some oil company profits are so big
they are really quite obscene.
Yet they keep gouging the public
on the high price of gasoline.

If as a country we don't get serious
about an alternative energy source
things will go on in the usual way –
oil companies in charge of course.

Each day it's becoming obvious
oil is more trouble than it's worth.
Let's regulate the regulators
and don't let fools destroy our earth.

Mishap In The Gulf

Offshore oil drillers in the gulf
were in a bit of a hurry.
They had a little bit of a mishap
and told the world it need not worry.

They claimed one thousand barrels a day
was all the oil that leaked away.
When compared to the size of the sea
it was about like spilling a cup of tea.

But when large oil slicks started showing
their loss estimates started growing.
It then soon became quite obvious
that some petrol folks had lied to us.

It was soon plain for all to see
an environmental catastrophe.
Oil folks took responsibility
and promised clean up of beach and sea.

They promised to clean up every drop,
if they could make that gusher stop.
Now, thanks to some educated fools,
once precious crude oil lies in pools.

Now it's of little use or worth.
It's just polluting Mother Earth.
All just because they drilled in haste,
they've laid Gulf Coast wetlands to waste.

A Really Crude Awakening

When the off-shore oil disaster
happened in May, two thousand ten.
Our country started thinking on
what a tricky spot we are in.

Yes, it's a crude awakening
when that crude oil comes ashore.
Today they clean up what they can
knowing tomorrow there'll be more.

There'll be oil on every shore and beach
within the big gulf water's reach.
And every wetland, marsh and slough
will be blessed with that sticky goo.

When Congress calls them in to testify
it tends to send them into shock.
But we have learned, they're more concerned
about the folks who buy their stock.

They're less concerned what the public thinks,
but terrified when their stock price shrinks.
It doesn't seem to matter what they spoil
they just want to get that precious oil.

Instead of sorrow over wetlands lost,
they'll be more worried 'bout clean-up cost.

A Really Crude Awakening (cont.)

If the MMS* and the Good Lord's willing
they'll keep on doing off-shore drilling.

For it's a fact of life, like it or not,
we need all the oil the gulf has got.
Let's regulate the drilling on land and sea
so the wildlife and wetlands will always be.

But let us hope the regulators
will keep a very watchful eye.
So greedy fools don't spill oil in pools
causing our coastal wetlands to die.

And at Orange Beach, at the Flor-a-bama,
if there's no mullet for the mullet toss,
have the National Tar Ball Championships
so that it won't be a total loss.

*MMS = Metal and Mining Sector

Wasted Water, A Wasted Way Of Life

He's a Louisiana fisherman
and has been all his life.
He commercially fishes every day
to support his kids and wife.

Now, thanks to a massive oil spill,
his livelihood is gone.
He hopes that things get better
but that gusher gushes on.

The spill has wasted coastal wetlands
and all the wildlife in its reach.
The fishing grounds are all spoiled
and ugly crude oil ruins the beach.

He's too proud to ask for charity.
He wants work to feed his kids and wife.
But thanks to careless greedy men,
wasted water wastes a way of life.

Unconcerned about what all they spoil,
they think of massive profits most.
They're hurriedly drilling deep for oil
and devastating our Gulf Coast.

Federal regulators and oil CEOs
had a cozy relationship some suppose.

Wasted Water, A Wasted Way Of Life (cont.)

Some say it was almost incestuous
and it's made a mess for the rest of us.

Someone seriously needs to watch the store
so this will not happen anymore.
Close regulation is the solution
our world doesn't need more pollution.

The Great Debate

By his silver tongue and well-chosen words,
he has been elected many times before.
But now his constituents have noticed,
he has lobbyist friends galore.

Now the voters just are not so sure
that his stated goals are all that pure.
Career politicians are not so popular anymore.
There is little doubt on that score.

Many feel it's detrimental, all that political clout
and the time is right to throw the rascals out.
Nowadays most every voter knows
trouble results from political pros.

Our country's condition is a sin,
but still they want our votes to win again.
They think they're indispensable
But they're retirement would be sensible.

His upstart amateur challenger
lacks experience and that is good.
For he is still honest and unconnected
and may do what he says he would.

An old incumbent experienced Senator
who has long been living like a Prince

The Great Debate (cont.)

On hearing some want him to be unseated
he won't be that easy to convince.

Yes the longwinded career politician
will loudly talk debate and shout.
But a new breed of determined office seekers
may just put the old pros out.

Then when the new politicians are in too long,
eventually it will sound like the same old song.
When they too learn that old political dance,
vote them out, give new talent a chance.

Understanding Politics

When you talk about politics,
I find it hard to understand.
When they will spend ten million,
for a job that pays one hundred grand.

But I guess they must like the limelight,
and being up there in control.
But claiming they love doing public good,
just doesn't seem to soothe my soul.

When they talk of their accomplishments,
when they start with all that bragging,
do they think I am illiterate?
And rode in on the turnip wagon?

When they start talking all that trash,
on their frantic campaign ride,
it makes me start to wondering
what all they have to hide.

Their reputations oftimes precede them
thanks to their public relations man.
But seldom will you find a candidate
that doesn't have a better plan.

It seems when they talk of their careers,
it seems it almost never fails.

Understanding Politics (cont.)

They inadvertently forget some facts
and some relevant small details.

So, before they start handling public funds,
there is one thing that should be required.
They should undergo a background check
before the voters say they are hired.

Lest we put a fox in charge of the hen house,
or a hungry hound to guard the meat,
let's learn all the nitty-gritty
before they're elected to some cushy seat.

The Political Game

All through our Nation's history,
it's always been the same.
If you want to get elected,
you must learn to shift the blame.

Get proficient at pointing fingers,
make your opponent seem low and mean.
While you play the part of good guy
and come out being squeaky clean.

But if you don't win the election
and pictured your opponent as a jerk,
you might have to do as millions do -
get a real job and go to work.

The idea of working for a living
is not well received, I will report.
The thought of working for a living
would be a Politician's last resort.

Yes, I have great faith in our system
and here is the main reason why -
I think we have the best Politicians
that money could possibly buy.

Yes, some folks say that crime don't pay,
but there's one fact they've neglected.
Crime does pay, in a real big way,
but it costs so much to get elected.

Coming Close

Coming close does count in horseshoes,
A-bombs and a manure fight.
But coming close don't count in politics,
those who have lost, know I'm right.

No matter the speeches made,
or talk of the things you've done.
When all the votes are counted,
you either lost the race or won.

No matter all the dollars spent,
no matter how high the cost,
the thing that really matters is,
if you won the race or lost.

No, coming close don't count in politics.
Those who have lost, know I'm right.
Coming close only counts in horseshoes,
A-bombs or a manure fight.

Voting Absentee

Way up in Cook County, when it comes election
day,
there are words of encouragement that politicians
always say:
"Folks, vote early and vote often, on this election
day,
and remember the special provisions, how to vote
when you're away."

You can just fill out some papers, we'll do it if you
can't see.
Your vote will count like you are here, it's called
'voting absentee'."
Along about election time, the precinct people work
long and hard
doing thorough voter registration, through most
every graveyard.

They see that all participate, in these big electoral
fights.
Just because the voter is away, he should still have
voting rights.
Just because they're resting, in their final resting
place
doesn't mean they can't participate, in a big political
race.

Voting Absentee (cont.)

If you don't think they can do it, just you wait and
see.
For with the proper paperwork, they will all vote
absentee.
So, when it's time for that long dirt nap, time for
that final ride,
To be laid to rest in Cook County is what many
folks decide.

The absentee list keeps growing, not shrinking as
some might fear.
For there are lots of voters' names added to these
lists each year.
Most choose to stay, to be laid away, for they love
political fights.
If you're not buried in Cook County, you may lose
your voting rights.

The Good Side Of Deep Snow

It is indeed an ill wind,
that doesn't blow some good.
Could deep snow help our Government?
Yes, I think perhaps it could.

Far away up there in DC,
the bad weather is not ending.
While everything is all shut down,
they're not in session spending.

In a place where words and money flows,
at times as fast as rockets.
Politicians are at a standstill,
with cold hands in their own pockets.

Though some think the DC winter
is about as bad as it could get,
if things stayed closed a few more days,
it could reduce our National Debt.

Yes, when you think about it,
bad weather can help a lot.
They ain't up there spending,
money our Country hasn't got.

Perhaps it's not a bad thing
to have a Legislative pause.

The Good Side Of Deep Snow (cont.)

We have overspent on money
And do we really need more laws?

So, if the snow storm is long lasting,
and the deep snow doesn't end,
don't think of snow as your enemy,
just consider it a good friend.

Yes, it is indeed an ill wind,
that doesn't blow some good.
Could deep snow help our Government?
Yes, I think perhaps it could.

Too Many Snouts In The Trough

There were so many candidates
trying to speak at the Great Debates,
causing one old commentator to scoff
"There's too many trying to get their snouts in the
trough."

If some of the Founding Fathers had their way,
they would serve only one term with no pay.
That's the way it would make real sense -
doing public service, at their own expense.

On another thing they would insist,
there'd be no such thing as a Lobbyist.
These people do have a bunch of nerve;
the only 'special interests' should be the voters they
serve.

Those in office should be made to understand,
their main concern should be the good of our land.
They shouldn't campaign on company time.
They are being paid by the taxpayer's dime.

Those office holders that feel indispensable,
should slowly walk through any graveyard.
And while they are taking this leisurely walk,
they should really think long and hard.

Too Many Snouts In The Trough (cont.)

It was an election, not a coronation.
They were elected to serve the Nation.
They were seated in office to do the voters' will
and they should not dip from our Treasury's till.

Most do enough damage just serving one time
by their reckless spending of the taxpayer's dime.
Many feel our country would be better off
with far fewer snouts in the public trough.

Campaign Promises

A woman been married ten years
still had not made love.
Here's how she told it to me:
Her husband, a Politician,
felt his primary mission
was just saying how good it would be.

A Politician through and through,
easier to promise than to do,
years later his political career ended.
A Politician through and through,
his promises never did come true,
with his pretty wife still unattended.

The Obscene High Of Campaign Costs

If the money spent on political campaigns,
was diverted to ease our Nation's pains,
perhaps to feed our Nation's poor,
where we're doing little and should do more.

And if these funds were used another way yet,
It could make a dent in our national debt.
Rather than re-elect many who are quite inept
and others who make promises that are never kept.

Now there is some talk of a billion dollar fund
to finance an important big campaign.
That's a big bunch of American dollars to spend
in the midst of much confused financial pain.

What if there was a limit on campaign spending?
Perhaps this insanity would suddenly end.
Why not put a thirty day limit on campaigns?
This would save so much political wind.

Then they could spend more time in DC
and take more care with our money they spend.
And worry more 'bout Government business
instead of when their terms will end.

Who makes the huge donations, is my main
concern.
For some big organizations have money to burn.

The Obscene High Of Campaign Costs (cont.)

When this happens, election results are skewed.
That's when the common voters get screwed.

When they talk of a billion dollar campaign
in times with an economy so lank and lean,
the thought of a billion dollar campaign
quite simply borders on being obscene.

Fiscal Restraint

The government needs to exercise some fiscal
restraint.
They spend money like it's there, when it ain't.
Yes, it always looks great and good on paper
But it often disappears like a cloud of vapor.

The dreamers can project a pipe dream surplus.
Most times it's enough to get some folks elected.
But then oft-times, it all comes back to bite us,
when the cash does not come in as projected.

I say, "Enough of these rosy projections
just to help politicians win elections!
Starting here and now, just let us end it!
When the money does come in, then we'll spend it".

But with each new administration, it's the same.
They can't seem to quit playing that guessing game.
I could project myself as a millionaire,
but it won't come true if the money ain't there.

Printing paper don't help if the economy is in the
tank.
And checks don't do any good, 'til they clear the
bank.
We need to exercise some serious fiscal restraint,
stop spending money like it's there when it ain't.

Fiscal Restraint (cont.)

Every time they start the printing press,
it complicates our financial mess.
Everywhere we hear the same complaint.
They're spending like it's there, when it ain't.

Front Cover Of The CAGW's* "Congressional Pig Book"

He's a champion pork producer,
and has been for quite a spell.
He's on the front page of "The Pig Book"
and is on the centerfold as well.

He's well liked by his constituents.
and is so very well connected.
If he keeps providing big-time pork,
he will surely be re-elected.

Now, the way he's spending money,
sometime it gets quite scary.
He acts like all the money comes
from the 'proverbial Money Fairy'.

He's the darling of his district.
He always fills their needs so well.
As long as they get their goodies,
the rest of the land can go to hell.

They've all been taught by their mothers,
"Kids, get along, play well with others."
But now, as long as they get theirs,
It's "Forget the rest, who really cares?"

But now the main plan is two-fold
and he's the Rep they have selected.

Front Cover Of The CAGW's* "Congressional Pig Book" (cont.)

As long as he provides the pork,
he is bound to be re-elected.

*CAGW = Citizens Against Government Waste

The Bucket And The Hog ~ Part 1

Back when I went to college, I was on the football squad.
I planned to go professional, and then really make a wad.
The Coach gave us our orders, said we'd have to hold the line.
Their biggest meanest quarterback was the one he said was mine.
He came running at me glaring, like he hated me the most.
I said, "Now friend, there ain't no way you'll reach that goal post."
When he finished tromping on me, I was flatter than a frog.
That's what happens when you stand between the bucket and the hog.

Then I went in the business world, the world of high finance.
I soon became a real big wheel, by work and luck and chance.
Then came the boss's son-in-law, with his heart set on my job.
I said, "Sonny Boy, there ain't no way, no sirree bob"
Then he used some J.R. tactics, like on the "Dallas" show.

The Bucket And The Hog ~ Part 1 (cont.)

He got promoted over me, and how, I'll never
know.
Now, I'm no longer a big wheel, I'm just a tiny cog.
That's what happens when you stand between the
bucket and the hog.

I guess every man nowadays, is familiar with
divorce.
I was gonna split so fairly, down the middle, why of
course.
The way I had it figured, we could both live pretty
good
if everything went the way that we both knew it
should.
Then she hired this young Attorney, with eyes like
dollar signs.
I said, "Ain't no way I'm gonna pay a settlement he
designs."
They took the kids and house and cars, they even
took my dog.
That's what happens when you stand between the
bucket and the hog.

I outfoxed the IRS; I thought I done it pretty
shrewd.
In American terminology, I was sure I had 'em
screwed.

The Bucket And The Hog ~ Part 1 (cont.)

I claimed some big deductions, all of which I was so
sure.
I knew my scheme was foolproof, so American and
pure.
They called me in for audit, and said a bunch I'd
have to pay.
I looked the tax man in the eye and said, "Man,
there ain't no way!"
They flattened out my bank account, like it was
rolled on by a log.
That's what happens when you stand between the
bucket and the hog.

I finally started seeing things, just how our country
ticks.
So I went out and got involved in modern politics.
I soon became a power, as politicians say,
and pretty soon most everything was going just my
way.
Then came a special interest group, bent on my
resignation.
I told 'em all where they could go, with little
hesitation.
Well, they toppled me like I was choked on that
dense L.A. smog.
That's what happens when you stand between the
bucket and the hog.

The Bucket And The Hog ~ Part 2

There are lot's of things in life that you never want
to do
I know there are many, but I will mention only two
Never ever try to pet a mean old junkyard dog
And take care that you don't stand between the
bucket and the hog.

The petrol spokesman said, "Sir, I resent your
personal attacks."
"We are barely breaking even, stop confusing me
with facts."
"Now these record quarterly profits, well sir that is
just a myth,
That's a portion of the money we are re-investing
with."
They're baffling us with B.S., as thick as L.A.
smog.
That's what happens when you stand between the
bucket and the hog

They made record breaking profits, more than ever
before,
but they cut back on maintenance, trying to make a
little more.
Because of those cost-conscious fools, precious
crude oil lies in pools.
their pipes became corroded, public confidence
eroded.

The Bucket And The Hog ~ Part 2 (cont.)

Alaskan oil stopped flowing, like a great big sewer clog.
that's what happens when you stand between the bucket and the hog.

The oil companies are re-investing many million bucks a day.
they say we'll ruin the scheme of things, if we get in their way.
Sorry that we cussed 'em, we've got to learn to trust 'em,
and try to overlook the fact they're taking most of our pay.
Now I've heard so many alibis, my mind is in a fog,
that's what happens when you stand between the bucket and the hog.

The petrol spokesman claimed they were barely breaking even.
Now that's the part I had some trouble in believing.
Now I don't mean to doubt their word, but I think it quite absurd.
They gave four hundred mil to a CEO who is leaving.
I guess I'll write about it in my personal daily log.
That's what happens when you stand between the bucket and the hog.

The Bucket And The Hog ~ Part 2 (cont.)

My blond neighbor lady ain't the sharpest knife in
the drawer,
but I'd have to say she was looking good, the last
time that I saw her.
In an act of desperation, at the local filling station,
she made a scene, and sold her car to pay for
gasoline.
You can read all about it on the daily news-web
blog,
that's what happens when you stand between the
bucket and the hog.

The Bucket And The Hog ~ Part 3

There are lots of things in life that you never want to
do.
I know that there are many, but I will mention only
two.
Never ever try to pet a mean old junkyard dog,
and take care that you don't stand between the
bucket and the hog.

A large chain of filling stations owned by gouger
offshore oil
got to where they are today through American sweat
and toil.
Now they're re-investing billions and nothing could
be finer.
But they're investing all the money in the Middle
East and China,
now our economic outlook looks flatter that a frog.
That's what happens when you stand between the
bucket and the hog.

The oil people say that they are having it quite
rough.
With all their corporate skills, they can't seem to
make enough.
I sympathize with those guys, I sympathize a bunch.
But if they don't cut me a little slack, I can't buy
tomorrow's lunch.

The Bucket And The Hog ~ Part 3 (cont.)

Yes, they've flattened out my bank account like it's rolled on by a log.
That's what happens when you stand between the bucket and the hog.

Great Grandma had an electric car, way back in nineteen three.
She had to buy no gasoline, and her car was pollution-free.
Now when I think about it, some things must be amiss.
After all our years of progress, we have come to this???
It makes me want to shout about it to some DC demagogue.
That's what happens when you stand between the bucket and the hog.

I don't smile much lately, the reason that I'm scowling
my Motor City Monster gets but ten miles to the gallon.
With all of our technology, we sent people to the moon.
You'd think we'd get more mpg, and get more pretty soon.
I feel like I'm the whipping boy, the one they always flog.

The Bucket And The Hog ~ Part 3 (cont.)

That's what happens when you stand between the bucket and the hog.

Now I've been using plastic money, I've been fueling with a credit card.
Now I think I've overdone it, the mini-payment is getting hard.
At the pumps today they took my card away – it was all maxed out.
I need cash for gas today. Either that or do without.
Now they're whipping me economically like I'm sinking in a bog.
That's what happens when you stand between the bucket and the hog.

Who Is Gonna Bail US Out?

When our Government needs more money,
they go and borrow from across the pond.
Those folks are generous lenders.
It's as easy as waving a magic wand.

Then the Chinese wondered when,
they would get their money back.
We said, "These are troubled times"
"Could you just cut us a little slack?"

"We will repay our debt, but just when,
there's just no way of knowing,
and rather than default on debt,
we'd rather just go on owing."

Our deficit just keeps on growing.
It's tends to make one yell and shout,
"Just who the hell will come along
to bail the good old U.S. out?"

The U.S. has been so generous.
We have given so much in foreign aid.
Many once poor starving nations
are now rich and have it made.

But perhaps it's time to change our ways
until our economy sees some better days.
Let's concentrate on our nation more,
rebuild our industries, and feed our own poor.

We Are All In This Mess Together ~ Part 1

The other night, the President did speak to all the
Nation
all about the economy and fuel conservation.
He said we'd have to watch it, or things would
worsen yet.
Then they loaded up the limousines in the
Presidential Jet.

Oh, we are all in this mess together.
We'll all have to suffer just the same.
Oh, we are all in this mess together,
and we'll all have to share in the blame.

Buy American, be American, help our balance of
trade.
Make sure it's made in the US, don't buy foreign
made.
Well, we all talked it over and we really liked the
plan.
Then we noticed that the brochure was printed in
Japan.

Oh, we are all in this mess together.
We'll all have to suffer just the same.
Oh, we are all in this mess together,
and we'll all have to share in the blame.
The high gas price they're asking is 'cause crude
price is climbing.

We Are All In This Mess Together ~ Part 1 (cont.)

Well, the trouble is Alaskan - talk about imperfect
timing.
The Alaskan pipeline has some leaks, yes, we'd
better all get braced.
Repairs will take many weeks, this could be the
worst we've faced.

Oh, we are all in this mess together.
We'll all have to suffer just the same.
Oh, we are all in this mess together,
and we'll all have to share in the blame.

They cut down on the chemicals, they were trying to
cut their cost.
Now all that precious crude oil floats on the
permafrost.
They let their pipes get rusty, trying to make a few
more bucks
Now it's going to cost us more to fuel our cars and
trucks.

Oh, we are all in this mess together.
We'll all have to suffer just the same.
Oh, we are all in this mess together,
and we'll all have to share in the blame.

We Are All In This Mess Together ~ Part 1 (cont.)

Yes, we are oil addicted, but addictions can be beat.
It's the same with everyone, all up and down the
street.
The future looks dark and murky, we all need to quit
cold turkey.
Tell the oil merchants to take a hike, we'll all walk
or ride a bike.

We Are All In This Mess Together ~ Part 2

We're all in this mess together.
We'll all have to suffer just the same
We're all in this mess together,
And we'll all have to share in the blame.

Gouger offshore oil said they would explore.
They would search the world over and try to find
some more.
They said that they could start real soon and all that
it would take,
was for our leaders to give to them just one more
big tax break.

My neighbor is one crafty guy; he lives by work and
sweat and toil.
Now he's running his old diesel car on old used
cooking oil.
You'll know it when he's been here, it should come
as no surprise,
the air is filled with the fragrance of onion rings and
fries.

When you talk about the economy well, you know
it's none too good.
When our President works weekends at his ranch at
chopping wood,

We Are All In This Mess Together ~ Part 2 (cont.)

and his second-in-command has been seen
throughout the land.
He was toting his trusty shotgun; he's hunting food
we understand.

I drove down to the filling station to buy a tank of
gas.
I was talking to the guy next to me, we had some
time to pass.
He said he hated the high gas price, he thought it
was a bummer.
I agreed and filled my Geo, and he filled up his
Hummer!

We're all in this mess together.
We'll all have to suffer just the same.
We're all in this mess together,
and we'll all have to share in the blame.

I'm Afraid The Good Old Days Are Coming Back

I remember Mom and Dad
talking 'bout the times they had;
how things were back in the good old days.
Where they went, they went by walking.
And they spent their evenings talking,
fixing food from the garden that they'd raise.

Now I'm back to walking
and I spend my evenings talking,
and weekends cutting firewood for my stack.
I don't know how to play it.
And I kind of hate to say it,
but I'm afraid the good old days are coming back.

Now I remember when,
if you were really in,
the symbol was a big old Cadillac.
Now it's how good a wood stove you've got,
and how much lawn is garden plot,
and a tiny car with no room in the back.

Now I've heard this old nostalgia kick
'til it almost makes me sick.
They like things like they were way back then.
If they want to live like Daniel Boone,
they're gonna have their chance now pretty soon,
'cause the good old days are coming back again.

I'm Afraid The Good Old Days Are Coming Back (cont.)

Yes, I remember Mom and Dad
talking 'bout the times they had;
how things were back in the good old days.
Where they went, they went by walking.
And they spent their evenings talking,
fixing food from the garden that they'd raise.

Now I'm back to walking
and I spend my evenings talking,
and weekends cutting firewood for my stack.
I don't know how to play it.
And I kind of hate to say it,
but I'm afraid the good old days are coming back.

Full-time Part-time

Like millions of Americans, I was recently let go.
I had to try, to just get by, but how I didn't know.
I finally found a part-time job, then I found another.
Then I took up dumpster diving with a Union
Brother.

Now I'm a full-time part-time,
I'm as lucky as I can be.
I used to have just one job,
Nowadays I'm working three.

Now I'm no longer unemployed,
so many jobs, I'm overjoyed.
I'm a lucky man considering my age,
but the jobs all pay minimum wage.

Now I'm supervisor of a crew, on which all of
whom
spend their days just like me, pushing on a broom.
It's an honest way to work and even earn some cash.
On another of my jobs, I'm the one who picks up
trash.

Now, I'm a full-time part-time.
I'm as lucky as I can be.
I used to have just one job.
Nowadays I'm working three.

Full-time Part-time (cont.)

Now I'm no longer unemployed,
So many jobs, I'm overjoyed.
I'm a lucky man considering my age,
But the jobs all pay minimum wage.

I have just received a rather big promotion,
It's a lucky break, and I guess I'm on my way
They gave me a key to the executive restroom
I only have to mop and clean it twice a day.

You may think working three jobs,
is about as good as it gets.
But you don't get enough hours,
to qualify for benefits.

It's true, working full-time part-time,
can really drive you up a wall.
But better having three small paying jobs,
than unemployed and no job at all.

I Have Outlived All My Savings

Now I cannot cater to my cravings
For I have outlived all my savings
Now I don't donate, I'm not giving
I'm in a different style of living.

Since my incoming interest fell
You could say the economy went to hell
We no longer have a cocktail hour
Since the stock markets all turned sour.

But there's lots of things one can do
I'm learning to make my own home brew
Now my old muscles will soon harden
For I'm out working in my garden.

I don't know which politicians to thank
Now I get my groceries at the local food bank
I worked my job since I was a pup
Now my pension plan's went belly up.

When I think back at the taxes I've paid
I'm glad it's being given for foreign aid
Giving foreign aid is hard to understand
Wouldn't it be wild to help our own land?

I'll soon park my car, and give up driving
I'll have to learn the art of "dumpster diving"

I Have Outlived All My Savings (cont.)

Yes, I once was in two pension plans
Now, I'm picking up aluminum cans.

Now, I don't donate, I'm not giving
I'm in a different style of living
Now I cannot cater to my cravings
For I have outlived all my savings.

The Litter Box Of Life

Working for a living for my kids and my wife,
just scratching around in the litter box of life.
There's something about it that does not seem quite
fair.
It seems that the fat cat gets more than his share.

It seems that the fat cats end up with the most.
Like they do the scratching, and I am their post.
But if it were not for me, they wouldn't have crap.
While I do the scratching, they're taking a nap.

The fat cat's on top, like he's always been.
Where I scratch in the box, the litter is thin.
If I could scratch up the cash, I'd pack and be gone.
That can't happen, so I just keep scratching on.

The fat cats scratch in the better parts of town.
All I get is the leavings, what little dribbles down.
If I could reverse things, if I was in their place,
I'd be the happiest cat in the whole human race.

The fat cats better hope that the rest scratch on
or their privileged places could soon be gone.
For now, I'll keep scratching in the litter box of life
working for a living for my kids and my wife.

I Still Have The Biggest Part

I started out with damn near nothing.
Yes, that's how I had to start.
I started out with damn near nothing,
and I still have the biggest part.

Yes, way back when, once upon a time.
I was headed for the top of the heap.
Though money was very hard to make,
I found it even much harder to keep.

So, long story short, now I must report.
I've slid back to where I got my start.
I started out with damn near nothing,
and I still have the biggest part.

But as I'm reflecting on this tonight,
at least I must have done a few things right.
For looking back to how I got my start,
I'm lucky to still have the biggest part.

The Ballad Of Bad Bernie Madoff ~ Part 1

Some investors begged old Bernie
to get on his investor/client list.
He wouldn't agree to work with them
until they really did insist.

Some investors made tons of money,
but there were many that never did.
You see, it always works out better
for those at the top of the pyramid.

They idolized old Bernie
as if they were in a mental fog.
They didn't realize they stood between
the bucket and the hog.

The SEC took a look at Madoff,
but they found nothing wrong
Heck, Bernie was a good old boy,
they had known him all along.

But when his admiring investors
had finally found him out,
In comparison he made Jesse James
seem like a tenderfoot boy scout.

You'll never find one greedier
than this old scheming dirty dog.

The Ballad Of Bad Bernie Madoff ~ Part 1 (cont.)

That's what happens when you stand between
the bucket and the hog.

To those that had dealt with Madoff,
the hurt and sting still lingers.
When you shake hands with old Bernie
you had better count your fingers.

Yes, Charles Ponzi was an amateur
compared to this old evil devil.
Bernie took the Ponzi scheme
to the next much higher level.

Bernie was a big-time business wheel.
A client is just one tiny cog.
That's what happens when you stand between
the bucket and the hog.

The Ballad Of Bad Bernie Madoff ~ Part 2

When they arrested Bad Bernie Madoff,
he did not offer to resist.
They talked to him quite harshly
and slapped him on his wrist.

His high dollar, white collar
crimes were oh so very bad.
So they put him under house arrest
in his high-rise penthouse pad.

His huge cash flow would soon go.
He was in one big financial bog.
That's what happens when you stand
between the bucket and the hog.

After the excruciating pain and anguish
of being confined in his pitiful pad,
his case did finally come to trial,
and his day in court was had.

He received a lengthy sentence
to an executive crimes facility.
There were no electric golf carts.
You have to walk to the starting tee.

Held in this place with no computer,
he has to write in his daily log.

The Ballad Of Bad Bernie Madoff ~ Part 2 (cont.)

That's what happens when you stand
between the bucket and the hog.

Bernie's reputation preceded him.
He was quickly recognized by all.
Now he's surrounded by many friends
in the reformatory dining hall.

He now has some 'Mafiosi' buddies
and they reminisce about old times,
and tell stories of their glory days,
with endless tales of their past crimes.

But they all have one thing in common –
bank accounts flatter than a frog.
That's what happens when you stand between
the bucket and the hog.

The Ballad Of Bad Bernie Madoff ~ Part 3

Many of bad Bad Bernie's ex-clients
learned from this big-time business whiz
when a deal seems too good to be true
most times that's exactly how it is.

They won't forget Old Bernie Madoff.
They remember him quite well.
How he handled their investments
and simply blew them all to hell.

His clients all believed him
like their minds were in a fog.
That's what happens when you stand between
the bucket and the hog.

Madoff went to a corrections facility
especially for the criminally "elite"
It's a gated community in the country
and is actually quite cool and neat.

To be sent here, one must have some pull.
This comfy place is most always full.
It lacks some amenities, I'm sad to report;
the residents must walk to the tennis court.

The inmates get their best exercise
when they run, or walk, or jog.

The Ballad Of Bad Bernie Madoff ~ Part 3 (cont.)

That's what happens when you stand between
 the bucket and the hog.

The other guys all look up to Bernie,
for he was so good at what he did.
Bernie built and ran the best scam ever.
He's called 'The King of the Pyramid'.

It's so good when one is idolized
by ones close friends and peers.
And most members of this 'elite group'
will be housed here for many years.

Many folks will long remember
this old corrupt investment dog.
That's what happens when you stand between
the bucket and the hog.

The Ballad Of Bad Bernie Madoff ~ Part 4

One rule for good investors is to diversify.
Bernie believed in this and would always try.
He earned a reputation as a big business whiz.
But, many times your money ended up as his.

He handled investments for those 'in the know'.
They trusted Bernie with their portfolio.
Like leaving a hungry hound to guard the ham,
the fact was that Old Bernie ran a scam.

Some saw their flow of money slow.
Then, one day it seemed to clog.
That's what happens when you stand between
the bucket and the hog.

Many saw their investment portfolio
never seem to lose, and grow and grow.
Now there's an old saying that is often true
Figures don't lie, but liars can and often do.

Sometimes he wouldn't accept new clients.
Old Bernie had this bit down to a science.
He'd play hard to get, but he always did
put the newcomers low in his pyramid.

It's like a really kind dog owner,
being bit by his own dog.

The Ballad Of Bad Bernie Madoff ~ Part 4 (cont.)

That's what happens when you stand between
the bucket and the hog.

Madoff may yet build a business empire,
even though he resides inside the fence.
by handling investments for his inside friends.
It only makes good business sense.

Old Bernie could handle inmates' investments
in the same way that he always did.
But of course they'll come out better,
if they're at the top of the pyramid.

Yes, old Charles Ponzi was a piker,
compared to this old dirty dog.
Some people learned you just don't stand between
the bucket and the hog.

The High Cost Of Executive Expertise

They claim that they were working hard,
and really meant no harm.
That it was just a little downturn
and no real cause for alarm.

Some say they were so arrogant,
And that they had lots of nerve
But they all wanted their bonuses
They claim it's something they deserve.

Yes, 'Big Buck' bonuses at AIG
may tend to look a tad bit funny.
But if not for their skills and expertise,
They could have lost real big money.

Investment managers of their caliber,
are so extremely hard to find,
the perfect mix of money skills,
coupled with an intellectual mind.

So, let's do our best to keep 'em.
Forget the bail out and don't cuss.
Just sit back and wait and see,
What they're going to do for us.

We need to keep Execs like these,
do our best to see that they stay,.

The High Cost Of Executive Expertise (cont.)

And reward their financial expertise,
with bonuses, perks and extra pay.

So be patient and just wait and see,
what they'll do for an encore.
They lost quite a lot the last time,
next time they may lose even more.

Let's pay 'em those big bonuses,
try just to keep 'em on the staff.
Then maybe next, they can blow it all,
instead of just blowing half.

Alibis And Lies

Alibis and lies and creative accounting,
they claim they tell the truth, but the evidence is
mounting,
that they tend to bend the truth just a tad.
Now the public has the feeling they've been had.

The petrol companies' PR folks should win the
Pulitzer Prize
for their skill in writing fiction, and the way they
rationalize.
One can easily sum it up, and it won't take but a
minute.
It is a fact that oil is slick, and so are all those in it.

Alibis and lies and creative accounting,
they claim they tell the truth, but the evidence is
mounting,
that they tend to bend the truth just a tad.
Now the public has the feeling they've been had.

I feel robbed at the filling station; I have to pay any
price they ask.
These bandits lack the decency to even wear a
mask.
They'll tell you that the price is up for any handy
reason.
Last time it was the mid-east war, today its
hurricane season.

Alibis And Lies (cont.)

Alibis and lies and creative accounting,
they claim they tell the truth, but the evidence is
mounting,
that they tend to bend the truth just a tad.
Now the public has the feeling they've been had.

It's true that figures do not lie, but liars often figure.
They claim they're breaking even, but the profit line
grows bigger.
The problem is the terrorists who done the dirty
deed,
and there is not a single trace of 'unusual' corporate
greed.

Alibis and lies and creative accounting,
they claim they tell the truth, but the evidence is
mounting,
that they tend to bend the truth just a tad.
Now the public has the feeling they've been had.

A Tribute To Two Wranglers

From out of the West, came two of the best,
with voices like rolling of thunder.
Head wrangler 'Texas George', sidekick 'Little Dick',
well known as the 'Wyoming Wonder'.

They felt the country was needing some change.
These wranglers then quit riding the range.
They rode in to town and soon, by and large,
they'd been elected, so they took charge.

They settled in at the main ranch house
and real soon they both went to work.
They felt they had the world by the tail
and they intended to give it a jerk.

Some of their programs started off slow
and others just tapered off from there.
But soon there was pork for most everyone
and the public did not seem to care.

After a big bad round with some terrorists
came a huge problem about oil and gas.
These two wranglers would solve the problem
though it meant kicking some Arabic ass.

They claimed Iraqi oil would pay for the war
with such little cost to our nation.

A Tribute To Two Wranglers (cont.)

Those who worried 'bout a lengthy war
were promised a conflict of short duration.

Inheriting a big budget surplus,
thanks to skills of the last President
this surplus money worried these wranglers,
and soon it, plus much more had been spent.

Then a second war, as if one ain't enough,
much disapproval, things got kind of tough,
approval ratings fell, as sometimes they do,
sinking lower than proverbial 'whale poo'.

Feeling they had done, all the good they could do,
they saddled up their mounts and bid DC adieu.
Now these two wranglers are ready to ride,
some say they'll miss 'em, some can't decide.

They'll be leaving town with saddlebags filled.
Some folks are sad, while others are thrilled.
A thought for all, as they mount up and ride west,
men with their expertise can do the job the best.

These wranglers felt much satisfaction
concerning all the good things they'd done
And one of them said that was one mighty spread
for just us two old wranglers to run.

Extracurricular Activities

It's widely done by Governors and Senators
and Congressional people too.
Mayors, lawmen and diplomats,
just to name a few.

They love to live a double life
anytime they please.
Intellectuals commonly call it
'extracurricular activities'.

Extracurricular activities
are games they play anytime they please.
They work hard and then they party down.
In DC, it's this way all around the town.

Most are politicians, doing what they do best;
working all the angles to feather their own nest.
Some have set some records, some difficult to beat.
Many there could qualify as 'a bedroom athlete'.

Even when they are caught, most show little shame.
Most are really skilled in the art of shifting blame.
When asked by the voters to just please step aside,
they claim their innocence, standing there with
pride.

Extracurricular Activities (cont.)

They know enough on others, the missteps they've taken.
They can make a 'favor call' that will save their bacon.
Birds of a feather flock together, and they always will.
For the most part it's that way, up on Capitol Hill.

A DVD Dilemma
Subtitled: How A Homemade Disc Can Haunt

He was torn between two professions,
sometimes that's how things are.
He wanted to be the president,
and as well be a porno star.

Now, acting and politics are similar.
He could do both if no one would tell.
But like so many secret schemes,
this one didn't go smooth or well.

He was running for the oval office.
But he dropped from the race real quick,
when it was revealed he had co-starred
in a self-produced porno flick.

With his such obvious shortcomings
and total lack of staying power,
his sensuous documentary,
was certainly not his finest hour.

Some people then wanted to sue him,
it was publicized in one report.
But some theorized the evidence,
would never stand up in court.

His homemade movie would reveal,
he was mostly mouth, and no big deal.

A DVD Dilemma (cont.)

To flaunt his prowess seemed his goal,
and Viagra played a supporting role.

He consistently campaigns hard,
trying very hard to never fail.
He was just filming his adventures,
while out there on the campaign trail.

As a prize winning movie maker,
a Michael Moore he'll never be.
Just a politician documenting,
his exploits for the world to see.

When you make records, tapes or movies
so many times it comes to pass,
sometimes even long years later,
they tend to surface and bite your ass.

It's not fair he's catching all the flack.
But, it seems that's the way things are.
For he was not only the actor,
he was the producer and co-star.

Saturday Night SOB (Sunday Morning Saint)

He sits up close to the preaching
and loudly says amen.
He hopes the congregation
don't know where all he's been.

He hopes to avoid detection
for he's up for re-election.
And the slightest hint of moral scandal
would be more than he could handle.

He's working hard to show the world
he's something that he ain't.
He's a Saturday night SOB
and a Sunday Morning Saint.

He's been out cruising in his new Mercedes
picking up 'commercial ladies'.
He claims the only way he pays
is counseling to change their evil ways.

He testifies he's living right
but he lies with every breath.
If the Good Lord loved a liar
he would hug that man to death.

He's working hard to show the world
he's something that he ain't.

Saturday Night SOB (Sunday Morning Saint)
(cont.)

He's a Saturday night SOB
and a Sunday Morning Saint.

So far, he remains undetected.
Polls say he will be re-elected.
His district considers him a blessing.
They're not aware of his cross dressing.

If his constituents knew the truth,
there would be hell to pay.
But he'll stay in their good graces
as long as he sends pork their way.

He's working hard to show the world
he's something that he ain't.
He's a Saturday night SOB
and a Sunday Morning Saint.

The Way It Seems To Be At The SEC

There is something in our government
that makes me quite forlorn.
The regulators at the SEC
were busy downloading porn.

Instead of watching big time brokers
and collecting financial facts.
They were watching porno flicks of hookers
that were performing sexual acts.

They were doing this on company time.
For some, 'twas their obsession.
Their minds were in another world
as we came close to a big depression.

As for me, I would much prefer
that they watch porn on their own time,
and not at work in our government
paid for by the taxpayer's dime.

I think this would be much better
and, yes, make much more sense.
Go ahead and get their "jollies"
but not at government expense.

Web Surfing At The SEC

Watching financial stuff on the computer
was sure becoming quite depressing.
So they started surfing on the Web
which soon became a real big blessing.

They resorted to Web surfing
just trying to cure the 'blahs'.
They soon clicked onto a site
that was full of 'oohs' and 'aahs'.

They soon were hooked on erotica
and girls with uncovered boobs.
Meanwhile, our financial world
had started going down the tubes.

Then as the stock markets tumbled,
and the Dow came crashing down.
They fiddled around like Nero
as he watched his burning town.

Things got so bad, the hard drives filled.
They had to download some stuff to disc.
There were rules against work time porn,
but it all seemed worth the risk.

With the financial world in disarray,
They were downloading porn every day.

Web Surfing At The SEC (cont.)

Amid sensual sounds of moans and groans,
'twas hard to hear the ringing telephones.

Oh, but now those days are done and over.
The SEC has promised to improve.
And you can be sure these regulators
are watching Wall Street's every move.

Attorneys With Ambition ~ Part 1

My nephew is an attorney
way up in New York town.
His law practice was doing great,
but nowadays it's really down.

He was conferring with a client,
when so horribly by chance,
he got painfully backed over
by his client's ambulance.

Now he's suing the ambulance company
and the EMTs as well.
For due to their gross negligence,
he'll be laid up for quite a spell.

In college he earned a law degree.
It hangs on his wall for all to see.
And when his college costs kept mounting,
he also studied acting and creative accounting.

You'll see his ads on TV.
Call his number if you have a case.
He will fight them all, big or small.
He can practice law most anyplace.

His firm stands ready to help you.
You only need to pick 'em.

Attorneys With Ambition ~ Part 1 (cont.)

Then, like a pack of junkyard dogs
all you need to say is, "Sic 'em".

You don't need up-front money.
There's no initial fee.
He'll get his from the recovery.
Just how much, you're gonna see.

Attorneys With Ambition ~ Part 2

He's suing another restaurant chain,
for that's where the money's at.
They neglected to tell his client
burgers and fries could make him fat.

Due to their inept gross negligence,
the client's homebound and does languish.
He lost his woman and his acting job,
and suffers stress and mental anguish.

In one case our attorney will handle,
his client was badly burned by a candle.
He wasn't warned of dangerous flame.
We have sued the store, they are to blame.

Now, a store was very negligent.
Not warning the husband or his wife
of the potential laceration hazards
concerning a real sharp knife.

Now, the husband cut his finger
and excruciating pain does linger.
On his behalf, we're suing that store,
for he'll have a knife phobia evermore.

Now he's suing a big fast-food chain.
He's going to take 'em down a notch.

Attorneys With Ambition ~ Part 2 (cont.)

They should have warned his client
that hot coffee could burn his crotch.

He says, "To all our critics who have cussed us,
we will keep on pursuing justice.
If our client's been badly treated,
we will get a sympathetic jury seated.

And much like the hero Robin Hood,
we will continue doing legal good.
Crusading for client's rights evermore,
robbing from the rich, giving to the poor."

Thanks To Our Attorneys

We owe so much to our Attorneys.
This truth we need to understand.
Were it not for our Attorneys,
we would live in a lawless land.

In the past, those guilty of Capitol Crimes
would soon have been put to death.
But thanks to skillful Attorneys,
we shelter them 'til their last breath.

Even when murders are committed
before a great big audience,
they very often beat the rap
with high-dollar legal defense.

He has some real good Attorneys
And, for him, they work for free.
For the people that pay their taxes,
will pay that Defense Attorney's fee.

The poor victims of this inmate
for a longtime have been dead.
But we continue caring for him,
keep him warm and clothed and fed.

The inmate keeps on eating and living
and his physicians keep him well.

Thanks To Our Attorneys (cont.)

And we pay for those who guard him,
though he is guilty as hell.

There are too many others like him.
And many folks are less than thrilled,
for the efforts of our Attorneys,
have our prisons and jails filled.

Yes, we owe so much to our Attorneys.
This truth we need to understand.
Were it not for our Attorneys,
we would live in a lawless land.

Success At Last

I once tried to be a writer, back in my younger years.
I longed for recognition, applauding in my ears.
But, it seemed my greatest efforts, were all to no avail.
I grew accustomed to rejection slips, in my morning mail.

Ah, but then one day I noticed, it was clearly evident,
Some writers were successful, most everywhere they went.
They became my inspiration, I too, a success would be.
Then I did some in-depth research, for the best approach for me.

Now, I'm a successful writer, I am widely read each day.
My works are read for miles around; folks believe the things I say.
No, I'm not in print in tabloids, nor appearing in great hall,
For I write my words of wisdom, on the restroom walls.

Success At Last (cont.)

My case is not uncommon, it's far too
commonplace.
It is a real strange malady, it plagues the human
race.
For far too many writers, are in print and in great
halls.
When in truth their works are suited for use on
restroom walls.

Other books, e-books, and audio books from
Jim Hubler
available at Amazon.com and Barnes & Noble

The Cliffs of Leavenworth
Some Trucking Tales (Volume 1)

**And don't miss Jim's music available
on CDs, DVDs, and mp3 format from
Amazon.com and cdbaby.com**

Mud Slinging USA, Volumes 1,2 &3
Pet A Dog ~ Help A Dog
Ballad of a Diesel Doctor
Boy, I've Backed A Rig More Miles
Trucking Between The Tracks
Beer, Cheaper Than Gas
I Ain't Worried About Retirement
The Devil's Convoy
Beginner's Luck

About The Author

Jim Hubler (William James Hubler Jr.) is a former Hoosier, now living in Kentucky along the beautiful Ohio River. After many years as a Trucker who played in Country Bands on the weekends, he is now retired and doing what he always wanted to do - write.

He has been writing songs for many years, now he has recorded several of them, with the help of some very talented friends. A few years ago he started writing his first book, and now has written three, with more in the works, and coming soon. As well, he writes some Poetry, 'Part-time Poet', thus this book.

Jim's interests are many and varied. He likes dogs, big trucks, good guitars, and writes about everything he likes, plus more. He loves the humorous side of life, but also writes some things 'as serious as a heart attack'. His main rule of life is, "Never Trust A Man That Don't Like Dogs."

www.ingramcontent.com/pod-product-compliance
Lightning Source LLC
Chambersburg PA
CBHW072023040426
42447CB00009B/1712